A DOG'S BEST FRIEND

Dog Training for Real Dogs and Their People

By Mila Johansen

A DOG'S BEST FRIEND

Dog Training for Real Dogs and Their People

By Mila Johansen

Published by Books Boost Business

Cover Design: Laura Helen

Book Production: Margaret Jean Campbell

Photo of Mila Johansen by Sandy Brooke

Produced in the United States of America

ISBN: 978-1-913501-20-4

Chapters

Meet the Stars of this Book

Chapter 1

Am I a Dog Whisperer?

Is there a nicer feeling than being in a room full of people and the dog chooses to come sit next to you? I think not.
~ Anonymous

I think most of us are in tune with our own dogs. For some of us that extends to other people's dogs, as well. Sometimes, I will visit a person who has a dog and as soon as that dog sees me, she runs up to me and we are instantly connected. I always wonder, does this dog sense I am a "dog person"? My ego would like to think so. Or is it more basic than that--she smells my dogs on my pant leg. Or maybe she is just a social dog by nature and comes up to every visitor with a greeting. I've even had dogs run up to me with a stick or a ball to throw and are delighted when they find a willing playmate who never tires. Usually, they peter out before I do.

But I do know that I speak out for dogs like I am doing now writing this book. Besides, I have mastered panting like a dog, which makes dogs totally love and connect with me. Arf.

I have been known to actually stop my car and speak out for an animal that I can see needs help. Or I will leave a note if I felt intimidated or not sure how my suggestion will be received.

I remember a period of time when I drove by a home that had a dog in a small kennel--about 4' by 6'. I drove that route for years and always felt sick inside to see the poor creature there day after day, year after year. I finally stopped long enough to take down the address. I sent a letter. I felt safer sending a letter. I told them that a dog can be a man's best friend and that maybe they should spend a weekend putting up a fence so their pet could have a yard to roam around in. I'm not sure of the outcome of that brave deed, because soon after, I didn't drive that route any longer.

My dogs only want one thing from me--my attention. Oh, and food. Two things. Dogs are the best "people" to do things with. They are always ready. They don't need to get ready. They don't have any belongings to bring. They are always willing. If I woke up at 3:00am, they would be glad to meet me at the door. They never complain about how long we walk—it probably isn't long enough for them. They never tire. They usually run up and down a trail at least twice for my once. They never complain about the food I serve them. They never complain about anything. They never argue with me. They just look happy to see me and are eager to do anything. The perfect friends!

***National Dog Week is the Last Full Week in September
NOTE: Full list of National Dog Holidays at end of book

Chapter 2

Could My Dog Survive Without Me?

What a childhood I had – I was ten years old when
I found out Alpo was dog food.
~ Rodney Dangerfield

I am a firm believer in teaching your dog to beg at the table. Not crowding you, or jumping on you, but waiting patiently for you to drop bits and pieces. Why? I will tell you why. Free clean up. Just kidding, but partially true.

I come from a family of survivalists. We store food and in doing so, we have to think about storing food for all of our animals. One thing we have learned is that you can't store too much at a time because dry dog or cat food will eventually go rancid. Canned food has a definite shelf life. We always have at least a three month supply on hand and then keep restocking.

Sometimes I wonder what would happen if we didn't come home, or we were gone when a fire started, and couldn't return--or any such scenario. How would the dogs survive? A little foraging could go a long way.

One of my dogs has discovered a sweet and tasty weed that grows around us, Miner's Lettuce. Princess Luna runs around grabbing huge mouthfuls to munch. I am so pleased to see her discover a food source on her own.

Later, she discovered the small, sweet grapes that drop to the ground below our vines. I know, I know, dogs are not supposed to eat grapes. But she does and I can't stop her. So far, she is doing fine with them. Recently, I discovered her foraging the dried-up blackberries on the thorny over grown bushes. I tried them. Yummy and sweet. A good food source in case of emergency. Thank you, Princess Luna!

Okay, now for the gross stuff. We live on a ranch and there is a plentiful supply of wild animal droppings that my four dogs love to devour when I'm not looking. I don't know why. They get fed plenty of food. So why do they choose to ingest that awful excrement left by our wild visitors? A mystery I fear I will never solve. Extra nutrients? Instincts left over from ancient ancestors living in the wild? Oh well.

And then there is the throw up left by our indoor cat, Angel. It's like dessert to them. I try to wipe the vomit up before they find it, but often they beat me to the draw. I suppose I should look at it like having a cleanup crew. Less work for me. But, ugh--yuck!

Now, two of the dogs have just begun their foraging in a new place--the kitchen counters. Who says you can't teach old dogs new tricks--or perhaps I should say, they taught themselves. For some reason, my dogs have developed some bad habits late in life. They have also begun rummaging through the trash and tearing it apart--a totally new activity that they didn't discover until later in life.

One of my dogs, Clementine, started digging for moles and gophers. Some days, she will catch two or three of them. Often, she eats them, getting plenty of nutrition. Other days, she just plays with them. We try not to pet her on those days to not get contaminated. By the way, my husband, a farmer, is very pleased to see the rodent populations diminished.

We had a cat many, moons ago, who loved to catch mice and give them to my husband, Rich, as presents. We called him Skyboy because he had one blue eye. Whenever Rich returned after a few days away, we'd open the bedroom door to find three--always three--rodents lined up on the floor. Gifts to Rich. Skyboy would only leave the gifts when Rich was home, thank goodness, so they were definitely presents for him.

PARK
RIVER
WALK
RANCH
FOOD
TRUCK
SIT
STAY
TREAT

Chapter 3

How Many Words Can A Dog Understand?

If you think dogs can't count, try putting three dog biscuits in your pocket and then give him only two of them.
~ Phil Pastoret

In my early twenties, I remember reading about Koko, the gorilla, in National Geographic. I became fascinated with Koko and began following her progress with her language skills. I think her word count was about 100 back then; words that she could understand and communicate through sign language. She ended up with more than 2,000 words.

So, I had the bright idea to teach my two dogs of that time period, Kuna and Rima, words. They were especially intelligent dogs--sisters. I have found that when you raise siblings from the same litter, together, their emotional intelligence is higher than that of single dogs.

In the end, I wrote down over 100 words that they knew and would respond too.

To Name a few:
Truck
Blue Truck
Silver Truck

In the Truck

Out of the truck

Park

River

Ranch

Walk

Bike

On the Bed

Off the Bed

Food

Go

Stay

Sit

No!

Speak

Go to bed

Stay

Hamburger

Yes, I said hamburger. Whenever we were in transit from one farm to another, we would stop at McDonalds and get each of them a plain hamburger--taking off the pickle. I must clarify. I only bought two hamburgers--one for each dog. I personally didn't eat at McDonalds. I have been, what I call, a "red meat vegetarian" for decades now--ever since college.

The reason isn't religious or anything like that. It began because, in college, chicken cost half the price of red meat, and I lived on a very modest income. So, at the end of the school year, that next summer, I bought myself a roast beef sandwich and after a few bites doubled over with severe stomach pain for two hours. I never ate red meat again. After nine months without eating it, my stomach juices refused to digest it.

The irony of that story is, I married into one of the last remaining slaughterhouses in Northern California. Again, my dogs, Kuna and Rima, became the beneficiaries of that situation, as the only thing I ever got from the accompanying meat market was bones for them.

Anyway, we would be about ten minutes from a McDonalds, and I would begin saying the word "hamburger" and the two dogs would flip out with excitement. We would stop for the purchase and they would devour the entire delicacy, bun and all. I got great enjoyment out of telling the window clerk the meal wasn't for me, but for my two dogs. Kuna and Rima exhibited the same excitement for three other words: park, river and ranch--all places they loved to run and swim.

Now to answer the question . . .

ENCYCLOPEDIA
OF FRANKLIN

Chapter 4

Can Dogs Really Speak?

Dogs do speak, but only to those who know how to listen.
~ Orhan Pamuk

Our dog, Franklin, is a prolific speaker. He actually tries to form words, just like he hears us do, and goes on and on with great expression. I am convinced that he thinks he is speaking just like us. Once in a while I imagine I hear a real word or two.

Franklin is what I call "a natural leader." He leads from behind without bullying or threats. He does the cutest, smartest thing: he waits at the door after a walk and greets each of the other three dogs as they pass in. He grunts a word to each and then follows them into the house.

Then when he thinks it's time to eat, he runs up to us and begins a very loud diatribe. When he sees us move towards the food, he gathers the other dogs, telling them "dinner is served" with his speech patterns. Franklin is extraordinary and highly intelligent.

I began making such a big deal of him speaking that two of the other dogs, Princess and Flower. His two sisters, seeing the attention he got, began mimicking him. So now whenever I say, "Are you speaking?" All three dogs go off. It can get rather loud, but I am so proud of their efforts.

***National Dogs in Politics Day is always September 23

Chapter 5

Quick Potty Training Tricks

It wasn't me, honest.
~ Princess Luna

Of course, there are the usual potty-training techniques you can look up online. But here are a few I have used, out of desperation, when raising three puppies at once.

Our dog, Clementine, got pregnant through the chain link fence of her dog kennel. The neighbor's dog came over and when we weren't looking . . . did the deed. She was young, barely a year old-- not the timing I would have chosen--if at all. She was due to be fixed, but we were waiting for the opportune appointment.

Clementine ended up having eight—yes, I said eight puppies, quite common for medium-sized dogs like her. My daughter and I were at home when she began the process. So, we brought in the small blue kiddie pool we had outside and put a quilt in it for her to settle into. We anxiously watched as each baby slid out and promptly named them anything we could think of. Franklin looked just like a brown and white guinea pig so, we dubbed him "Guinea Pig".

We didn't think we would be keeping any of them since we already had three other dogs. They were destined to go to good homes. So silly names were passed out freely. Princess. Who would name their dog Princess? Eight puppies landed on the quilt while Clementine looked proud and confused. Then came the bloody placenta and then . . . SUPRISE! One more slid out about half the size of the others. *Flower* . . .which made nine puppies.

After the required time nestled next to their mother, we found that a handy place to keep nine puppies for containment and easy cleanup was the bathtub. At eight weeks, we began the process of locating suitable homes for each. One problem. We had decided to keep one puppy. But . . . each of us, my daughter, my husband and I had become attached to a different puppy, and none of us would give up our favorite. So, we ended up giving away six of the babies and keeping three.

Note: We actually made a very short contract to give to each prospective owner so that we could be certain the puppies went to good homes. We even put in a clause that if for any reason, they could not keep the puppy, they would return it to us to give away again.

When all was settled, we struggled with potty-training three puppies at once. We don't leave our dogs outside at night, too loud and besides, in our house, they are a major part of the family.

I have found that procuring used quilts is the best way to create beds on the floor for my dogs. They wash easily and are comfy. I go to thrift stores to find the sturdy, no batting quilts sewn with vertical squiggle lines. They wash more than a hundred times successfully, compared to those with batting that would only last through forty or so cycles. I tried dog beds, but they didn't wash well and could be torn up easily by gnawing puppy teeth. With quilts, I can wash them once a week or more often as needed.

It seemed that each night, one or more of the puppies would have an accident. At that time, we were feeding them two meals a day--morning and night. So I came up with the idea to just feed them in the morning. That did the trick. By the end of the day, they had eliminated all their excrements and we began sleeping through the night--all of us. Celebration! Of course, there would always be the occasional accident.

Okay, I can hear some of you saying that you feel sorry for a dog not getting a decent dinner. One vet I know explained to me that canines in the wild can go for days without eating when they don't find food. It's in their ancestral make-up. Besides, I saw a poster in the same vet's office that showed two dogs. One was overweight and one was thinner. The thinner dog lived 5 years longer than the overweight dog. I came home changed that day and began feeding all of my best friends a little less. Princess had been getting bigger around her girth and just by giving her barely less, trimmed her right down, adding years onto her life.

Note: I now try and remember to give each dog ½ of a rice cracker each evening. Even I feel a little sorry for anyone not getting dinner. They look forward to the snack and that seems to give them some satisfaction.

Chapter 6

Vinegar
For Health and Clean Up

*Apple cider vinegar is so much more than a delicious addition to
a recipe. There are multiple health benefits from consuming and
applying diluted apple cider vinegar.*
~ Amy Leigh Mercree

As you can imagine, with four dogs, there can be a huge amount
of "accidents" or excess bodily fluids. There is enough of that
with one dog, but with four, it is sometimes a constant struggle--
especially out here on the ranch.

So, after the initial potty training, there might be a grace period
until they approach old age. Many single mishaps occur in between
but are easy to deal with one at a time.

Vinegar

One of my secret weapons is . . . vinegar. I take baby wipes and
douse them in vinegar--either apple cider or white. I have found
apple cider to be more effective. I keep the wipes on hand in the
original container. That way I always have a ready supply to wipe up
any quick events. Vinegar takes care of the smell and is an effective
cleaner.

Another reason I keep apple cider vinegar on hand is to add tiny bits into their water each day. Vinegar creates alkaline in their bodies and helps prevent cancer and outer skin growths. Since I have been adding vinegar to my dog's water, my current dogs have way fewer skin bumps and growths as they age. The most I ever put in is ½ -1 teaspoon in a one-gallon water bowl.

If you are just starting to put apple cider vinegar into your pet's water, be sure to just start with a few drops and add a little more each time. This way, they will get used to it and not go without water if the taste is too strong. Of course, the most important thing for your dogs to consume is water.

Please look up the benefits of vinegar on the Internet for yourself.

*Another secret weapon I have is to make a spray of lavender, rosemary and other essential oils. The right combo totally disarms any unpleasant smells immediately. This also helps repel ants and spiders and other creepy, crawly critters. Most rodents and pests are repelled by any kind of mint. Lavender and Rosemary are in the mint family. Look up ratios of Essential oils to water online.

Chapter 7

One Swat Lasts a Lifetime
And Could Save Their Life

*We have a saying in K9: "If you put three dog handlers in a room,
the only thing that two of them will agree on
is that the third is wrong.
~ Mike Dowling*

I can feel a disagreement coming on with at least some of you. As
part of the training, I usually give one quick smack with a loud
"No!" at least once when a dog is young. This is actually to save their
life in certain situations later, such as chasing cars, or an encounter
with a snake, or a multitude of other dangers. I did this with each
of our dogs when they were young and now all I have to do is grunt
loudly or say "No!" and they back off.

I've had two dogs kill chickens. Not a good habit to fall into
and one that could get them shot by neighbors. Once our friend was
clearing small trees and limbing bigger trees here on our ranch for
fire prevention. We were not at home. He witnessed our large dog,
Max, kill every one of our chickens in a matter of minutes.

This will sound severe to you, but I tied him up on the front porch for a month. I took him on a leash three times a day to relive himself. Max possessed an extraordinary intelligence and understood exactly what he had done. He never killed another chicken, of which we had many. We also had dozens of guinea fowl in the following years and Max guarded them rather than harming them. That extreme measure made Max a better dog and ultimately saved his life. We live around other ranchers and if a dog kills anyone's farm animals for any reason, they think they have the right to shoot your dog. Max lived for ten more years after this incident.

I have often heard of the punishment of tying the dead chicken around a dog's neck. But I just didn't feel that would work for us.

One more extreme occurrence happened at a friend's house when Franklin, at a very young age, killed our friend's chicken. I know some of you won't approve, but I beat him that day and he never forgot it. But he also never killed another fowl. Luckily our friends were very lenient people and didn't demand a more severe punishment. But I knew we might not be so lucky with the next person.

Now, many years later, I had to give Franklin one more life-saving lesson. For some reason, after the age of ten, he stopped listening to me when we were out walking. He began going over to the woodpile where we know there to be the occasional rattlesnake. I called and called--nice voice, angry voice,-- I tried every voice even saying "treat". He wouldn't respond. So, after several days of this recalcitrant behavior, I picked up a small rock and threw it at him with a loud "NO!" It hit him right on the top of his head. He jumped in surprise and ran back to me. Now whenever he moves near something I don't want him around, I just have to bend down and pretend to reach for a rock and he immediately changes course. He is a quick learner. Once was enough.

You can use essential oils with your pets,
but be very careful and study positive and adverse affects first.
Each essential oil contains dozens of therapeutic compounds.
These compounds have a much stronger healing potential than a
whole plant. That's why it's important you don't just pick any random
oil to use on your dog.

Please look up online to learn more.

Chapter 8

The Magic Spray Bottle

To chase a dog is merely to teach it to run away.
– Eric Knight

Dogs hate to be sprayed—at least most dogs. I have a spray bottle ready at all times. If they go near an area I don't want them to—one quick spray and they back off. In fact, finding this out later in the game makes me think I could have used the spray bottle instead of the swat along with a loud "No!"

Your spray bottle can do double duty as a bug deterrent by adding in a few drops of lavender essential oil. PLEASE look up essential oils and your pets. I have used them ***very diluted*** for years with my pets and have had no problem. I think it is because I use very small amounts. Lavender is one of the safest and most non-toxic oils.

Again, I have several spray bottles around so I can find them easily. The ones that work best are the ones with a long shot spray option.

Disclaimer: There will always be the one dog that actually likes to be sprayed or ignores it completely and is not deterred. But that dog will be rare.

Chapter 9

Yikes --I Forgot the Collar---Now What?

There's a world of difference between a dog that is off the leash and a dog that is trained to be off the leash.
~ Don Sullivan

I firmly believe that every dog should be taught to be on a leash without a collar. There are several reasons for this. I have found myself out walking with one or more of my dogs and have needed to restrain them.

We had to take the collars off three of our dogs when they started climbing over fences – six-foot-high wire farm fences. We were afraid they would hang themselves. So often, I am out walking and need to put a leash on one of them that I always carry one with me.

I have purposely taught each dog to be on a leash without a collar. I loop the leash through and put it on them. All have learned total restraint and walk without pulling or lunging.

I always think about if we were stuck somewhere and all I had was a sweater or a scarf. After this unusual training, each of my dogs would behave perfectly, tied to any makeshift leash, and ultimately be safe in any situation.

Chapter 10

Here a Leash, There a Leash, Everywhere a Leash

Some of my best leading men have been dogs and horses."
~ Elizabeth Taylor

So, now what about leashes? I leave one in every vehicle, a few by the front door, one in the bedroom and one in the green house.

I do the same thing with scissors and several other tools around the house and in the garden. I don't want to run and get every little tool when I need it, so I pepper them in all the convenient areas. I do the same with leashes. Sometimes when the UPS truck arrives suddenly, I don't have time to hunt up a leash. I have one in every area for an easy reach.

I buy several leashes at the dollar store and that way have plenty stashed around in case of emergency.

***National Walking the Dog Day is always February 22

Chapter 11

Bones for Teeth – Give a Dog a Bone
No Leathers or Rawhides

Everyone thinks they have the best dog.
And none of them are wrong.
~ W.R. Purche

One very wise vet told me that giving your dogs bones to gnaw on can keep their teeth in perfect shape—better than any procedure. Only the big beef bones. No ribs.

You may have heard that bones are dangerous for dogs. That pertains to cooked bones. Never give your dogs cooked bones. REPEAT after me – "No Cooked Bones!" They can splinter and choke them. I have found that I even have to pick up their old bones in the yard after they bake in the sun.

But raw bones are good for dogs. I try and give mine raw bones once a week. I don't always make that goal, so at least once a month.

Here is a story to reiterate how good bones are for a dog's teeth. Our dog Max was getting older at age fifteen. One day he took a turn for the worse and looked like he was going to die. I took him to the vet to see if there was anything we could do for him.

She said he would probably be dead by morning. But as she opened his mouth to look inside, I heard her gasp. "Oh my god--he has perfect teeth for his age." She stood there stunned. I told her about the bones and how my other vet suggested them.

Our dogs have never gone to the vet for any kind of work on their teeth.

Chapter 12

Make Them Love Their Kennel

Happiness is a warm puppy. ~ Charles Shultz

Kennel training is very popular with dog trainers and dog owners. And for most, that means the small or larger cage like apparatus with a door that hooks. I would like to caution you not to overuse your kennel.

When I speak about my kennel, it is a large one, 8 ft by 8 ft. since I live on a large farm. Our four dogs don't spend much time in there, but when I need to go away for short or longer time period, it is a safe place to put them. Due to "Top Dog" competition, only two of the dogs stay in the kennel. One dog stays in the house and Clementine, the mother, left outside to roam the ranch. Clementine has, for some reason, been resistant to training, so we let her wander free and do not try to contain her.

Expecting I would have to force each dog every time I put them into the kennel, I came up with some early solutions. I only gave them treats when time to enter the kennel. So from the beginning, they knew they would only get their treat in the kennel, which made them eager and created a race to see who would be first. Now when I say the word "cage", Princess Luna and Franklin run in and wait for me to close the door. We don't even have to give treats any more.

Franklin especially loves the kennel and herds Princess Luna into it or runs ahead of her and calls her to join him. He possesses a unique emotional intelligence when it comes to the other dogs. I think he loves being with his sister so much that he looks forward to time in the kennel with her.

In the beginning, he was always in there with both Princess Luna and Flower. But, we eventually had to separate the two sisters when they began a dangerous "top dog" competition that once in a while resulted in a major physical battle.

This training method can work for any size kennel. Our friend, Penny, has an extremely smart dog—a fluffy Pomeranian. When Sunny does something that needs punishment, Penny only has to say, "Time out." Sunny runs to his small kennel in the bathroom, faces out lying on his belly and waits until she tells him it's over. Personally, I think Sunny thinks it's a game, smiling his dog smile all the time.

NOTE: We do not leave any dogs in the kennel at night or they would bark. And we have our nifty quilt program on the floor that seems to work perfectly. For the most part, they all sleep through the night. Yay. Celebrate!

Chapter 13

Are You A Dog Whisperer?

Histories are more full of examples of the
fidelity of dogs than of friends.
~ Alexander Pope

Some people question their ability to be a good dog owner. Never doubt it—your new pet will train you. Ha, ha. And there is always the choice of professional training if it makes you feel more comfortable. There are tons of books, YouTube tutorials and advice from friends for you to tap into.

Dogs just want your attention. If you focus on their needs and play with them and walk them—Bingo!--you are a stellar dog parent. It's a great investment all around. You will have a superior companion who never argues with you, wants to do anything you want to do, and is always ready to go! You will have a guard dog or at least an early warning system.

My niece and her husband told me they wondered if they would make good parents. They finally tapped into their courage and got a dog. I told them right off that they would make great parents and/or dog owners. They found a Labradoodle who had been abused by being left long days in its small kennel cage. So, my niece found a

$1,200.00 dog for free through a rescue program. Turned out to be a wonderful dog and they both discovered the many perks of having a dog and that, of course, they could master it. In my opinion, every household needs a dog for unconditional love.

Their success with the dog encouraged them to have a child, which brought them ultimate joy and completion. Both, of course, are wonderful parents in every way. It always eludes me why training to be a parent--the most important job any of us will ever have--is not included in school curriculums. We are all left to fly by the seat of our pants, learning all we can from friends, books and trial and error. It's one of the great enigmas of life.

Chapter 14

Mutts Versus Pure Breeds--Rescues

A lot of shelter dogs are mutts like me. ~ Barack Obama

In our family, we prefer mutts, mixed breeds. Seems like the cross-pollination makes them smarter on all levels and less likely to get sick. Most of our canine family members came to us by accident, or kismet or serendipity, or divine intervention.

We've only had one pure bred—a small poodle. At one point in my life, we were between dogs and didn't have one for about two years. That had never happened to me before, and after about a year and a half without a dog, I began feeling like something major was missing in my life. Even though I am in a good marriage of many years and have a daughter at home, I knew then, I couldn't live much longer without the unconditional love of a dog.

I started looking around for the right dog. For a while, I thought it would just show up at the front door, or on our ranch as all our other dogs had. But after several months of looking out the window, I finally visited the animal shelter. We needed a small dog for the neighborhood we lived in. The woman at the pound said, they hadn't seen a small dog in over a year. So—don't judge me, I became desperate—I went to the pet store and rescued a poodle from the puppy mill. Yes, I consider the purchase a rescue. Peaches, a fluffy, peach colored small pure-bred poodle that cost me a pretty penny

If I would have known about the poodle or other breeds rescue program, I would have chosen that route. It wasn't until a couple of years after that I found out about those service programs. As I understand it, you can adopt almost any breed. They can come with problems from their previous home life. Or perhaps the individual or family merely found out that they couldn't keep the dog for some reason: moving, money, being too busy, other.

I have one friend who has rescued four Golden Retrievers who all turned out to be the best dogs ever. Each came with some problems, but with love, food and training, all became a central functioning part of the family. My friend found her last dog, Henry, emaciated, skin and bones almost dead on the floor of a kennel. She knelt down, looked into his eyes and knew he was supposed to come home with her and be her next canine family member. The woman at the rescue center tried to steer her to another healthier dog. But my friend is fairly intuitive and knew Henry to be her dog.

She brought him home and nursed him back to health with a diet of chicken and rice with plenty of water and love. Henry responded and grew to be a robust, strong dog who lived with his new family for over twelve years. I admired Henry as one of the smartest, most emotionally intelligent and almost human dogs I have ever known.

They don't dub poodles "The Einstein's of Canines" for nothing, as I soon found out. Too brilliant for her own good, Peaches turned out to be the hardest to train of all my many dogs. In hindsight, I should have sprung the bucks to take her to a professional trainer.

But now on to the best way to find the right dog.

***October is Adopt a Pet Month

Chapter 15

Do You Find Them or Do They Find You?

*Dogs have a way of finding the people who need them and filling an
emptiness we didn't even know we had.*
~ Thom Jones

First of all, I have to say--dogs are for life. And by that, I mean.
once you adopt or find a dog—it is a commitment for life—the
life of the dog. A wonderful symbiotic relationship that will enhance
and change your living standards for the better.

All but two of my multitudes of dogs found me. As a child, my
single mother taught school all day, and through a physical weakness,
came home and went to bed early, which left my brother and me
to fend for ourselves. I felt lonely and I desperately wanted and
needed a pet to love and hold. So, at first, my mother allowed me to
have a parakeet. I called him Pierre, a yellow bird with an apparent
personality. He rode around on my finger or my shoulder. But one
day, he flew off into a tree never to be heard of or seen again. So, we
went through a series of yellow parakeets, all dubbed Pierre.

Finally, my mother gave in and let me have a cat—Midnight. She fulfilled some of my cravings for a furry friend, and slept with me on my bed.

Later, as a teenager, an elderly neighbor woman gave us a Chihuahua, named Queeny who became my appendage and provided my first experience with the unconditional love of a dog. Now, as I write this, I wonder if that woman saw my loneliness and that's why she sent Queeny to us.

Later in life, after a series of other dogs, two amazing canine family members showed up on our ranch where my husband and I were working. They were dropped off with their mother, a golden cocker, and two brothers. Someone just dumped the mother and four eight-week-old puppies on the side of the road. How could they do that? But now I am grateful, or we wouldn't have found two of the most special beings on the planet to join our family.

At first, we thought we would keep one and give the others away. Back then, I preferred female dogs because they don't seem to run as far and tend to stay closer to home. So, I knew I would choose one of the two all-white females—one of the two sisters. We gave away the two brownish brothers, each to a different home. After that, we gave away the mother.

So, then it came down to which one of the white siblings to keep. One day, Rich assigned me the job of disking, tearing up the top layer of earth with a giant metal implement pulled by our tractor. Both white puppies started following me. One of them soon fell back and lay down under the shade of a peach tree while the slightly thinner one wouldn't relent. She never tired and after two hours, there she still ran, panting behind me. I knew then and there that she was meant to be my dog.

The next day, I found a nearby home for her sister. But within a day, she came back. So once more, we gave her away and she returned to us again. Finally, Rich and I looked at each other and knew we would keep both. We hadn't ever thought of having two dogs, but that turned out to be one of the best decisions of our entire marriage. We discovered that two siblings from the same litter, growing up together, made them smarter and more emotionally intelligent.

Kuna and Rima lived with us for seventeen years. They enjoyed swimming in lakes and rivers, following me on the tractor for endless hours, and made our lives before children fulfilled.

I learned about opposites from those two. Rich read an article that said in most families, children have opposite personalities. If there are two in a family, one will be outgoing and the other shyer and more reserved. This proved true with Kuna and Rima. Kuna outgoing and a little more aggressive badgered her sister, Rima, more reserved by nature.

Both Rich and I loved the dogs equally, but he naturally gravitated to Rima, while I related to Kuna. Later, I taught hundreds of children, many from the same family. I witnessed the truth about opposites in every group I worked with. It always proved true no matter what. So, when Rich and I finally decided to have a child, we only had one. She was easy and mild. We were afraid we might get the opposite child the second time around.

After Kuna and Rima, we had a dry spell without any dogs. A challenging time for me since I relied on my canine family members for fun and support.

But finally, another family of dogs showed up at our ranch and we found our next group of amazing canine companions that live with us now. Princess Luna who so reminds me of Kuna, Flower who I cannot live without and Franklin who is the leader and has become Rich's sidekick.

NOTE: Some of the best dogs are ones who have been owned for a few years by an older person.

Chapter 16

Fur Versus Hair

No home decor is complete without dog hair.
~ Anonymous

Dogs come in all shapes and sizes, some with hair and most with fur. There are advantages to both.

Many people who have allergies find they can live with dogs with hair. Another advantage to a dog with hair is they shed far less than a fur baby.

I will say, however, that the only dog we ever had who was a hair baby, our poodle, had to be washed if she got into any kind of grunge like mud, oil or muck.

Our furry dogs could come back to the house covered from head to toe, but as soon as they dried off, the debris would fall off them and completely disappear. Unless it was a dark oily material, there would be no trace of the offending substance as soon as they were dry. They would look fresh and clean as if they had just taken a bath.

Peaches, the poodle, on the other hand, would remain covered until washed. And living on a ranch, that was often. Poodles on a ranch, you ask? Yes, she loved the farm life as well as any other canine. She was just as talented at finding any messy substance to roll in. And we have to remember, poodles were first bred in Germany as hunting dogs, not in France as most people believe. Poodles were meant to run and frolic in mud puddles and retrieve the lifeless bodies of a hunter's success.

Fur babies shed like crazy. So one of our banes of life is fur balls--all over the house. My advice--leather furniture or vinyl. Repeat after me: *No cloth furniture!* I will say that in the future, I would love to find short hair dogs, so when they do shed, it's not as apparent. Of course, that probably won't work out in my dog style life, since I always seem to have my meant-to-be dogs appear out of nowhere.

<h1 style="text-align:center">Chapter 17</h1>

<h2 style="text-align:center">Running Extends Their Life—And Ours</h2>

If your dog is fat, you're not getting enough exercise.
~ Author Unknown

Most of our dogs live to be about seventeen years old. One reason is that they are not big dogs, but either small or medium-sized. Kuna and Rima each weighed about 35 lbs. But the big reason is running!

The main reason I feel our dogs live so long is running! I really believe that running extends their lives by three to five years. I have heard somewhere that exercise for humans does the same thing. I hope so.

I have a close friend who walks her dog a long way every day. The canine buddy gets her out to exercise. Years ago, her previous dog, Luna, kept her active with long walks every evening. Luna, a gorgeous, brilliant Springer Spaniel lived to the age of seventeen. When Luna passed, Penny stopped walking for a long period of time.

I told her what I tell everyone who loses their dog, "Get another one." She didn't believe me because Luna was the only dog she had ever known, and she didn't think any other dog could compare. For over two years, I kept at her to find another canine companion.

Finally, Penny took the plunge and found Sunny, a fluffy Pomeranian with a huge personality. Sunny got her out walking again, adding years to Penny's life.

A dog can cheer up anyone and add value to their life. **All dogs are the same.**

*****Canine Fitness Month is April**

Chapter 18

Are Dogs Smarter Than Us?

No matter how little money and how few possessions you own,
having a dog makes you feel rich.
– Louis Sabin

I'm beginning to think that we will never know how smart dogs really are. Just because they don't talk and speak words like we do doesn't mean they aren't smarter than us. They might be. Wow, what a profound thought.

They can do many things we can't. Their hearing is superior to ours. They are stronger than us and can run for hours. When we hike with our dogs, they run ahead and then run back to check on us. So, they often do the same trail two to three more times than we do, with no apparent fatigue.

My friend Penny treats her dogs almost like they're human. She expects them to achieve great things and both of her dogs, past and present, do amazing things. Luna, her previous dog, would take her many toys out of a basket, and then put them back into the basket when finished playing with them. Luna also opened the screen door with a string to let herself into the house.

Everywhere Penny moved, Luna would make friends throughout the neighborhood while Penny was gone each day teaching. She would make the rounds to each person's house for food and hanging out. One day as Penny and Luna walked down a nearby street, a woman called out and said, "Oh, is that your dog? She comes to sit at my feet every day while I write." Penny, surprised, soon learned about many of Luna's daily visitations around the neighborhood.

Penny's current dog, a fluffy Pomeranian, exhibits many of the same intelligent traits. Sunny, pulls Penny's socks off both feet each evening and picks out the shoes to be worn the next day and brings them to her. When time for a walk, Sunny disappears into the closet and reappears with the harness and leash. Sunny then jumps onto the footstool anxiously waiting for Penny to put the apparatus on him. I think her dogs do these amazing things because she expects them to.

Sunny loves games. Whenever Penny leaves the house to go somewhere, she hides about five small treats around the house for Sunny to find after she leaves. Sunny waits patiently by the front door and doesn't start until Penny is gone.

One time I sent a gift addressed to Sunny. He knew instantly it was from me from my scent on the item.   When on vacation at Penny's one summer, I discovered that Sunny loved a certain length of stick to cart around, and for Penny to throw out for him to chase.

On the drive back to Northern California, I stopped in a small town. On the lawn of the government building were several sticks just the right length. I gathered them up, rubbing my scent all over them, put them in a padded envelope and sent them to Sunny. Penny said he became very excited and knew they were for him even before opening the package.

I have been teaching Princess Luna to count. Yes—count. Every day the four dogs and the cat walk up and down the slight hill of my driveway four times. So a few months ago, I started looking into Princess Luna's eyes and putting up a finger for each time and saying the number.

She loves the lesson and comes to me for each count and knows at number four, we go back into the house. She can actually count to five now for when we do an extra time up the hill.

I have also named the doors of the house so they know which one to got to. Front door, back door, bedroom door and big door (the sliding door).

Great Pyrenees are huge white, long-haired dogs best known for guarding herds of goats and sheep. They are livestock guardians and happiest living outside with their flock.

During the recent fires in Northern California, the flames raged in the Napa Valley area. One family had to suddenly flee to save their lives. They left behind the Great Pyrenees who guarded their herd of goats. The fire was so hot, destroying everything in its path, that they never expected to see the dog or the goats again. After the smoke cleared and they returned to their home they looked around at everything still smoldering. Then through the mist came the large dog and all the goats. That Pyrenees herded the goats through the fire and saved every one of them. The family was astounded.

One article states that dogs are as smart as two-year-old children. Researchers have found that dogs are capable of understanding up to 250 words and gestures, can count up to five, and can perform simple mathematical calculations.

I say, we don't know how to measure their intelligence. Our own standards are too minimal and incomplete. We have to remember that Einstein was thought to be "slow" and did not do well in school. How could they have possibly known how to train a genius of the future? Same with dogs—we have no adequate measurements to know what they know.

Our poodle, Peaches, played the funniest, smartest game with our daughter who was ten. Olivia would hide from her while I told Peaches to wait with me. Then at a certain point, I told her, "Go find Olivia." She would search each part of the house just like a person.

Why she didn't sniff her prey out, I'll never know. She methodically searched each nook and cranny of every room before she finally located Olivia. We would play this for an hour or so. Both girl and dog loved every minute of it.

Chapter19

Top Dog

You can usually tell that a man is good if he has a dog who loves him.
~ W. Bruce Cameron

The psychology of our two dogs is intricate and we are not sure we understand it. Outwardly, it looks as if Princess Luna is the aggressor, herding and growling at Flower. At a certain breaking point, when Flower has had enough, she starts a major fight, and although half the size of her sister, is tough and will not relent. We have no way to separate them.

Nothing works, we soaked them with the hose, tried to pry them apart with a board, tried to pick them up. Scary. It has only happened three times in ten years, but each time, we feared one dog would kill the other. A few dog experts that we told all said they know of situations that are similar, where one dog did kill the other.

I do need to mention that most days, they are best friends, cleaning each other's ears, playing on the carpet, sleeping next to one another each night and so on.

Since paying attention to their growing animosity, we have mitigated their aggression. The spray bottle has helped with this.

I like dogs
Big dogs
Little dogs
Fat dogs
Doggy dogs
Old dogs
Puppy dogs
I like dogs
A dog that is barking over the hill
A dog that is dreaming very still
A dog that is running wherever he will
I like dogs

~ Margaret Wise Brown

Chapter 20

Free Feed Versus Control Feed

*A well trained dog will make no attempt to share your lunch. He'll
just make you feel so guilty
that you can't enjoy it.
~ Helen Thomson*

There are a couple of feeding methods that are constantly debated.
Free feed versus control feed.

We used to always have the feed bowl full for our two previous
dogs, Kuna and Rima. They never ate it all and so didn't overeat
with the free feed program. They would actually wait until night to
see if anything better came along, then they would chow down. Both
stayed nice and slim all their lives.

With our current dogs, we do control feed, mainly because we
have so many dogs and also to eliminate accidents during the night.
They do from time-to-time become overweight.

I asked our vet which method he thought best. He believes in
free feed. He also told me that in the wild, wolves and other canines
do not eat every day—only when they have a kill or find an animal
already dead. So, if our dogs did not have food for a couple of days,
for some reason—it really wouldn't hurt them.

In the same office, I saw a poster that changed how much I feed our dogs. It showed two dogs of the same breed, one overweight and the other a normal size. It stated that the slim dog lived five years longer than the overweight one. I found that to be profound and cut down the amounts we fed each dog

I did it in increments because I know when I don't want to eat as much, I eat smaller amounts and within a few days am not as hungry due to shrinking my stomach. Princess had been getting a little chunky and by doing this, she slimmed way down within a couple of months. I felt happy that I probably extended her life by 3-5 years.

I've heard of so many different kinds of feeding programs. Many sled dog owners create their own food for having multiple dogs by throwing everything into a pot and making a delicious canine goulash. I read an article about one man who put grains along with all parts of the fish he caught, with anything else on hand into a giant stew. The dogs loved it and it gave then strength for the powerful work they did.

Inspired by him, I often buy the cheapest package of boneless chicken I can find and combine it with brown rice for a scrumptious canine brew. I often mix it with half dry dog food. My dogs also love fruits and vegetables, especially apples, broccoli and red cabbage. Look up various food ideas for yourself on the internet.

Dogs are our link to paradise.

~ Milan Kundera

Chapter 21

To Swim or Not to Swim

Why does watching a dog be a dog fill one with happiness?
~ Jonathan Safran Foer

In my opinion, all dogs are meant to swim. At first our two previous dogs Kuna and Rima, as puppies, would not get into the river and swim with me. So, I swam over to the other side and stood on the bank. They couldn't stand not being with me, and after much howling and moaning, they both took the plunge and became my permanent swim partners. They loved it! We went swimming in the nearby river almost every day of every summer all seventeen years they graced our family.

Given the chance, most dogs will become the swimmers they are meant to be. Some may only splash in mud puddles. Some of my friends provide those small, blue kiddie pools for their canine to cool off in during the hot summer month. But most dogs, given the chance, will swim in lakes, river and even in the ocean.

My friend, Penny, has a friend whose business is to board people's dogs when they go away on vacation. She had an inground pool and often hosted a swim party for owners and their doggies. I fortunately attended one of these mixed company forays and found great delight watching the comical scene that ensued.

Even poodles are meant to swim. We think of them as "the fancy French poodle" when they actually originated in Germany as hunting dogs. They were bred to be water retrievers. The name "Poodle" comes from the German word Pudlhund. Pudel means "to splash" and "hund" means hound, which equals "dog".

So if you have a body of water nearby—let your pooch go for it!

***Many cities have Dog Swim Days in various pools.

Chapter 22

To Fix or Not to Fix

The lord in his wisdom gave us three things to make life bearable;
humour, hope and dogs. But the greatest was dogs.
~ Robyn Davidson

Should you neuter and spay your dogs? Of course, the conventional answer is "Yes!" Unless you are planning on breeding puppies for any reason.

My daughter and I rescued a multitude of animals over the years, mostly cats who showed up at our house—sometimes entire litters. We would give them away, but often got them fixed before finding them homes. In our area, there is often an organization who performs the act for free.

Our two white dogs, Kuna and Rima, each had a litter of puppies before we opted to get them spayed. I think that motherhood made them better, wiser dogs, even though our current dogs who were fixed before having puppies have very much the same disposition.

I must tell you a bittersweet story—well a humorous story in some ways. Our friend, Eric, has a working Border Collie—a brilliant dog who is a professional sheep herder. A champion, never fixed, left as nature intended, as a sire for other sheep dogs. *Tip* has fathered many champions and talented working dogs.

One day, he disappeared and couldn't be found. Eric made every effort over a three-month period and reluctantly gave up, broken hearted to lose his best dog.

About three months later, he saw Tip on a ranch he visited across the county. He whistled and called the dog who came to him with his tail between his legs. The other rancher told Eric that Tip had been living with him for the past months. He said, "You can thank me later for getting him neutered."

Eric, crushed that his champion breeder had been changed and rearranged forever, drove Tip home.

Chapter 23

Fleas and Ticks Begone

A flea can trouble a lion more than a lion can trouble a flea.
~ African Proverb

One word:

Frontline

I am a dedicated organic farmer who speaks out against the travesty in our society of spraying unnecessary poisons endangering our families and ourselves. I admire Rachel Carson for speaking out ahead of her time and quote her constantly.

But when it comes to fleas and especially ticks, we use Frontline. We've tried other ones that weren't effective. By now there may be some others that will work. But we live in tick country and have lost a couple of friends to Lyme's disease. So in that department, we are not taking any chances.

As precautions, we wear disposable gloves and don't touch the dogs for three days afterward. I even go so far as to open a plastic bag to throw the empty vials into, and use scissors only used for that activity.

Here's how it plays out. People try to tell me all the time that ticks are only out certain times of the year. Nope. They are around most of the year. The only time they seem to disappear is in August and September when it is totally dry here in Northern California. Then at the first rain, they are everywhere three days later—they appear out of nowhere.

Some years they are prolific. We mainly have the bigger turtle-looking ones, which are not supposed to be as dangerous as the tiny black deer ticks. But we aren't taking any chances—all ticks carry an assortment of bacteria and diseases. I try to give the dogs the Frontline every 4-6 weeks. On a big tick year, we find dead ticks all over the house when they fall off the dogs from the poison.

Before finding Frontline a couple of decades ago, we often had flea infestations. Since Frontline – no more fleas!

There are some organic alternatives and tons of flea recipes online, which use essential oils. But, *please*, be very careful using essential oils on your pets!!! You can use them, but very sparingly. No matter what the internet says, do not put essential oil drops on your dogs straight without a carrier oil or in a water spray bottle.

Repeat after me—"Never straight!!!"

Chapter 24

The Sneaky Dog

*You can trust your dog to guard your house but never trust your dog
to guard your sandwich.*
~ Anonymous

Do you have a sneaky dog? We do. Out of four dogs two of them have become sneaky as they grew older: Princess Luna and Flower.

Flower only sits in our chairs when we aren't looking. I know she is sneaky, because when she hears me coming, I hear her jump off before I can catch her. I have started putting a small empty box on each chair. I know many people allow their dogs on the furniture and I normally would too, if it weren't for the tick problem.

And we live on a ranch, in the foothills, where we have tons of raccoons and rodents who prowl around, outside our house, at night. We find their droppings as evidence of their visits. I don't feel that my dogs' paws are very clean to be sharing our living room furniture.

Princess Luna is another story. She has just discovered how to raise herself up to the counters to steal food. We keep the cat food on one counter. It's a higher counter by about two feet, but she is tall when standing on her haunches. She also tries to take our food too.

So now, I have to push everything away from the edge where she can't reach it.

When I catch her in the act, I give her the loud "No!" that accompanied that "one swat" when she was young. She slinks away, knowing exactly what she did wrong.

There is an upshot to "the sneaky dog." It proves they are smart. Super smart. It takes a brilliant dog to try and hide their misbehavior. Celebrate smart dogs!

When my daughter was a toddler, I read an article about how in Sweden it was against the law to spank children. They solved this by removing anything a child could reach that would be dangerous or get them into trouble. All breakables were put away and the houses were virtually emptied of any temptations. So I did much the same thing—I made my house child friendly. Our living room became a playground.

Chapter 25

Houdini Dogs

Every dog must have his day.
~ Jonathan Swift

As I've already said, my dogs learned new mischievous tricks as they got older. Princess started opening doors. She would reach up and simply push the lever-type door handle with her paw, and suddenly I would think someone had come into the house. Or I would enter the kitchen and the door would be standing wide open. She could go both in and out.

My mistake. One smart woman informed me that I should have put turn handles on all the doors—not levers. So I replaced all the handles leading outdoors, which stopped Princess Luna from opening doors and never closing them.

Then Franklin discovered how to open the huge sliding glass door. We were surprised when trying to keep him in the house, he would suddenly appear outside with all the other dogs following him. He learned to push that lever which only moves in and out and then slide the door open. A difficult feat which would have proven difficult for most dogs.

So, then this meant another trip to the hardware store where we bought a two-foot dowel rod to fit into the track that kept the door from opening. For a time, before we figured it all out, between Franklin and Princess Luna, they could open any door in our house.

I have a friend who used to have two Siamese cats. She and her husband would come home to every cabinet door in the kitchen open. The cats had learned how to even climb up to even the highest cupboards.

All but one of our dogs learned to climb our six-foot-high fence. As I already mentioned earlier, this was when we took all collars off the dogs so they wouldn't hang themselves.

Chapter 26

Yikes, I Lost My Dog!

Dogs are not our whole life, but they make our lives whole.
~ Roger Caras

I'm not sure I can write this next chapter. Well, here goes. I'll try. A few years back, Princess Luna got lost. It was one of the worst times of my entire life. I still shudder at the memory of it and can hardly speak about it. (List of how to find your dog at end of chapter)

I love all four dogs, but Luna happened to be the one I could take for bike rides and swimming in our local Yuba River. Each dog has something special I do with them. Flower stays by my side while I work outside. The others run off to explore all corners of the ranch.

Luna is the one I take places with me because, when they were all puppies, she turned out to be the only one who didn't drool profusely in the truck. So she, by default, became my river-swimming partner. Everyone loved seeing her follow me, swimming upstream to our favorite rock formations and short water rides. Over the years, Luna and I have spent hours at the river.

The day I lost her, I dropped her off at, my friend's house who is a dog groomer. I'm not normally a person who wants her dog groomed, but our dogs have way too much hair and it about four times a year, becomes a necessity. Jonnel's business is called "Groom With a View." A witty title referencing where she lives.

After putting Luna in one of the high-fenced kennels, I returned to my pickup truck and drove home. I soon received a call from Jonnel in a panic telling me that Luna had climbed the six-foot fence, pushed the lever on the door of the room and let herself out. She was nowhere to be seen.

My heart sank as I drove the fifteen minutes back to Jonnel's. We both searched the hilly neighborhood and finally Jonnel gave up to go back to work as I frantically called for my precious dog.

Since we live on 32 acres, I have developed calls for the dogs. Shrill calls that involve words like: treat, food, puppy, Luna. She must have heard my truck drive away and wanted to follow me. It was unfortunate that we had taken her collar off with the metal nametag with our phone number.

Poor Jonnel, she felt responsible. But how could she have ever suspected Luna to be a talented Houdini escape artist? Not only scaling a six-foot chain link fence, but also going to the door and letting herself out by jumping up and pushing down the lever handle.

I never gave up. After returning home to gather food and water, I returned to continue the search until dark. I knocked on every door and spoke to every neighbor asking them to look out for her. I called out for so long that I almost went hoarse. I traipsed through as much of the terrain as I could—even though I knew it was rattlesnake season. Jonnel finally called me into her house for a delicious quiche dinner.

I went home that night but returned at five a.m. the next morning to resume my search. After some hours I returned home to plaster info and pictures of her all over local Facebook community sites. I found a decent picture of her—not great. Listen to me –go right now and take some good pictures of your dogs. Don't hesitate—do it now. Hopefully you never have to use them in this way.

I typed up a simple sign and took it with the picture to the local copy shop and made 11 x 17" posters. I made it easy to read for passing cars. I posted them everywhere I could think of in the immediate neighborhood and for several miles in surrounding areas. I was relentless. Note: You'll need a staple gun and clear packing tape. The only tape that works is Scotch clear packing tape.

Before returning to Jonnel's, I went home to see if there were any Facebook results. I checked my computer one more time later in the day before returning to spend the night at the location. So many good Samaritans helped by reposting "the lost dog", which spread the word even wider.

I prayed that someone found Luna and was keeping her safe.
I feared she would run into the road or meet a rattlesnake or a
mountain lion or . . . the thoughts became too much for me. I even
went so far as to think how I could live without her. I tried to tell
myself, I still had three dogs at home and then I reasoned with
myself that having many dogs, I was bound to lose one of them to
something.

I called and called and called for her. I'm sure the neighbors were
weary of having me there, but most of them seemed very supportive.
I slept in my truck that night.

The next morning after calling for her over and over, I returned
home to check the internet. Success! Someone had spotted her on
a road several miles away down a major highway. I jumped into my
truck and drove to Melody Lane. Twenty minutes away, I prayed she
was still there. I inched down every part of the road, calling her name
through the rolled down windows.

I came to a place where I had to turn left or right. I went right
and drove as far as I could before turning around to try again. Then
I went down a road to the left--still calling, calling and driving super
slowly. Suddenly I looked in the rearview mirror and there was Luna,
frantically running behind the truck.

(Tears falling as I type this) I stopped the truck and got her in quick, before anything else could happen. She sat in the front seat panting, looking very relieved and disheveled. I gushed all over her, tears flooding my eyes, without touching her because of all the poison oak she must have traveled through.

We drove home. I've never let her out of my sight again. When it's time to get groomed, I go with her and help Jonnel with the process. I am so thankful every day to have my beloved Luna back. I hope to never have to search like that again for anyone. I'm not sure I could survive it.

I hope no one reading this ever has to go through that harrowing experience. just in case, here is a list of what I did. One local woman who speaks out for animals and helps owners find lost dogs, posted this list on her website. She was impressed by the measures I took to find my dog.

I made this list of all the things I did to find my dog, Princess Luna, so others can do the same things. Save in a file and share when someone needs it. Hopefully never.

1) I kept going back to the place she disappeared. I drove my truck slowly so she could hear me. She usually wears a collar with a name tag with our phone number on it.

2) We already have a loud, shrill call that she is used to here at the ranch. I almost went hoarse calling her for three days.

3) Drove & Hiked all over the area. I'm getting a dog whistle.

4) Posted on at least 10 local FB Community Sites Morning and Night. That is what got her found in the end. Someone recognized her from pic on FB. ***Didn't have a very good picture. Take pictures now.

5) Made Large Posters 11 by 17 and posted at every stop sign in area and on group mailboxes. Clear packing tape for metal poles. Stapler for wooden poles.

6) Talked to as many people in the neighborhood as I could and stopped cars to ask them to keep a look out and drive slowly.

7) Camped out where she was sighted. Left out food and water and her blanket with her smell on it.

8) ***Left someone at home on phone in case anyone called. They did!!! I went right over and found my dog.

9) Calls and Post to FB radio stations, Dog Pound, Animal Groups, (Contact & take posters to NID & Sheriff's since they drive all over the county)

ONCE SHE CAME HOME--I wept for hours

1) A tablespoon of wet food in bowl of water 3 times a day to hydrate

2) No petting due to Ticks and Poison Oak.

3) Rubbed her feet with aloe and lavender essential oil

4) Shoved garlic chunks down her throat in case of a snakebite or . . .

5) Let her sleep. She survived 3 days and 2 nights in the wild.

Chapter 27

Puppies Trainable at Ten Years Old

If there are no dogs in Heaven,
then when I die I want to go where they went.
~ Will Rogers

Over the years, I have come to the conclusion that most dogs are their very best around ten years of age. They finally reach maturity and are better dogs in so many ways.

Our poodle, Peaches, always the mischievous rascal, finally mellowed out at age ten. That is about when Clementine arrived and, within a year, gave birth to her litter of nine puppies, three of which we kept. Peaches became their nanny. She showed them how to do things, like jump in the pond and swim. She also became their babysitter at night. When one of them would start moving, she would grumble-growl at them instructing them to lay back down and go to sleep. She came in very handy at that point and we relied on her to perform certain caregiver tasks with the new additions to our family.

Peaches, the perfect older lady, would go into the bedroom and lay down at 8:00 every night. Even though, we never went to bed before ten, we could always find her there at that same time every night.

Chapter 28

When Not to Trust the Vet

I think to be a good veterinarian, you have to like people.
~ Kevin Fitzgerald

One day our older dog, Max, the one that came with the ranch years before, did not look well and was getting weaker and weaker. So, I took him to our regular vet who had gone away on a two-week vacation. He was out of town that day. A talented vet who could always get to the bottom of almost any problem with any dog. And the dogs liked him. He would get down on the floor at the beginning of the visit and sit right next to the dog—not something I've ever see another veterinarian do.

A woman came into the room, the veterinarian who took over in his absence. After examining Max, she told me he would probably be dead by morning and then went on to suggest an x-ray to see if it was cancer or any other serious ailment. I almost fell down when she came back with the quote of $800.00. This was several years ago so I'm sure it would cost more now. And besides, she already predicted "he would be dead by morning."

I told her that we could never afford that and especially since Max was 15 years old, a ripe age for a dog as big as he.

She got a little huffy with me and said, "This is the dog you have loved for so long and you should do everything you can to help him."

Then I asked her what she would do if the X-ray did show something serious. Without batting an eye, she told me she would recommend surgery, for even more money starting at $1,200.00.

With her still fuming and trying to talk me into the x-ray, I paid for the visit and left. Needless to say, I felt totally used and abused. Later, I realized that as an interim doctor, she tried to make some extra cash while sitting in for my regular vet. I couldn't think of any other possible explanation.

I tried to tell my vet about this later and didn't go back to that office for a few years. I found another veterinary office to take their place.

Chapter 29

Diet For The Fifteen-Year-Old Puppy

*Old dogs, like old shoes are comfortable. They may be out of shape
and a little worn around the edges, but they fit well.*
~Bonnie Wilcox

Max didn't die that night or the next morning. He lived an entire year longer. Here is how it happened.

I had heard from a friend on Facebook that he had extended his dog's life by feeding her cooked chicken and rice.

So, I went home that day, after the unsavory visit to the vet, and cooked up some chicken with brown rice. I gave it to Max mixed with half water. He lapped it up and by the next morning had partially recovered.

I gave him the same meal, chicken with rice and half water the next morning. He responded. I realized that he had probably been dehydrated. We continued the same meal from then on. Max didn't come all the way back to his usual vigor, but enough to run around the ranch with his youthful adventure mate, Clementine. She kept him going. She kept him in shape and inspired to keep on keeping on.

After that, we started feeding all of the dogs chicken with rice at least part of the time. Sometimes just to extend the dog food that is so expensive at the store. We have found that it is actually cheaper to cook a huge package of chicken with a lot of brown rice than to buy the 50 pounds of dog food.

We hope to extend the life of all our dogs with this wonderful diet. We always add water to every meal--even to dry dog food. I read somewhere that adding water to every meal saves their teeth also.

***November is Senior Pet Month

Chapter 30

Younger Dog for the Older Dog

Life is a series of dogs.
~ George Carlin

We found our dog, Clementine, on our citrus ranch. She came just in time to rev up our older dog, Max, who had been showing signs of slowing down. I am certain, she added at least three years to his life. They were partners-in-crime. She inspired him to keep on running all over the ranch for years to come.

Our best dogs have always been found on our citrus ranch in the valley. Kuna and Rima were dropped off with their mother, a golden cocker, and their two brothers many years before. We found the mother and two brothers' homes and kept the two sisters. They turned out to be the most incredible dogs ever and lived to be seventeen years old. The most incredible until we met the next batch who are equal in every way.

One day, we returned to the ranch to find a beautiful black and white springer spaniel with eight very young puppies. My daughter latched on to one that was entirely black and since we only had two dogs at home, Max and Peaches, we said she could keep her. But we decided to let the puppy have another two weeks with her mother.

About a week later, our ranch manager called to say that all the puppies with the mother had disappeared but, for some reason, Olivia's was still there. So, Olivia and I immediately jumped in the truck and drove the two hours to the citrus ranch and found the puppy still there, by herself, as if she were waiting for us.

We took her straight to a local vet to get shots before heading back up the hill to home. We told the vet about the mother and the other puppies and surprisingly enough, he told us that someone had brought in the mother with all the puppies that very morning. The same couple decided to keep the mother and all seven puppies. We were stunned, but happy at the news and, should I mention, relieved at such a positive outcome.

Olivia named her new puppy Clementine because that is one of the citrus varieties we grow. Clementine threw up all the way home.

I have a few friends who brought home a younger dog before their older dog perished. Always, the younger dog added years onto the elder dog's life and then became a comforting replacement when the time came to say goodbye.

One thing I have learned is that getting another dog is the best way to heal from losing your beloved companion. Some people don't believe me and say they will never have another dog as good as the one they just lost. But believe me, there are many great dogs out there just waiting to come home with you and give you that unconditional love and loyalty.

Dogs come into our lives to teach us about love and loyalty.
They depart to teach us about loss.
A new dog never replaces an old dog; it merely expands the heart.
If you have loved many dogs, your heart is very big.
~ Erica Jong

Chapter 31

A Valuable Lesson From Max

*The world would be a nicer place if everyone had the ability
to love as unconditionally as a dog.
~ M.K. Clinton*

At the end of his life, when he turned fifteen, Max started losing his hearing. I had no way of communicating with him except to push him in a direction or put him on a leash. I realized I should have started using hand signals a while back. I knew people used hand signals, but never thought to use them myself.

So, I began that day with the younger dogs so when they age, we will have a communication system set up. I don't even think I used the standard ones, just made-up ones that worked for me. I have two. One for "come here". One for "sit". You can look up the standard hand signals online. Start today.

Chapter 32

A Word About Cats

Owners of dogs will have noticed that, if you provide them with food and water and shelter and affection, they will think you are a god. Whereas owners of cats are compelled to realize that, if you provide them with food and water and shelter and affection, they draw the conclusion
that they are gods.
~ Christopher Hitchens

Most people think that everyone is either a dog person or a cat person. I believe that is true to a certain extent. I am definitely partial to dogs. I find life to be a challenge if I don't have a dog in the family at all times. Like I mentioned before, we experienced a two-year period without a dog in the home. It proved to be a terrible, desperate time until we found another canine companion. Living without that unconditional love put a dent in my normally positive disposition.

But at the same time, I enjoy cats. They are finicky, impervious to our needs and want everything to be done on their terms.

"Pet me until I scratch you."
"Don't pet me there, or I'll scratch you."
"Feed me now. Feed me now. Feed me now, Meow!"

"No, not that, I demand fancier food."
"I'll come to you when I feel like it."
And sometimes . . .
"See you in a few days/weeks."

Still, we live with them like the stand-offish boyfriend or girlfriend that because the harder they play to get, the more we want them. They are commanders of the game and we are merely their loyal subjects. Final answer.

Egyptians believed cats were magical creatures that brought good luck to the people who housed and fed them. These treasured pets were often dressed in jewels and fed meals fit for royalty. When cats died, they were mummified.

Archaeologists in Egypt have discovered mummified cats in many ancient tombs dating back more than 4,000 years. Ancient Egyptians believed cats held a special position in the afterlife.

Cats serve so many wonderful and useful purposes.

Soft, furry, pet-able (on their terms) comfort buddies
Low maintenance housemates
Fierce barn kitties that keep our outbuildings rodent free
Sometime healers when we are sick
Gopher and snake hunters
And they don't eat much!

When we first moved to our farm, the ground was riddled with mole and gopher mounds and trails. We ended up with about twelve cats and within two years, there wasn't one gopher mound left. We didn't see a rodent for years. We also have rattlesnakes. Rattlesnakes come around to eat the rodents, so with less food for them, we had less of the dangerous serpents.

Our cat population finally dwindled down to one, our cat Angel. We found her mother, Princess, namesake to the dog Princess Luna, on my husband's father's ranch years before. She showed up one day during our citrus harvest and my young daughter scooped her up into her arms and the rest is history.

Princess, the cat gave birth to a litter of five kittens while we were away on a two-week vacation. My daughter fell in love with the almost all white kitten with some black markings. We gave the other four away to good homes.

Princess proved to be an extraordinary cat. She sported six toes on each of her four feet. We were convinced that the extra toes required her to become an extraordinary pianist. Every morning, we woke up to her playing a deliberate twelve-note musical piece on the piano. Always just twelve notes.

Angel outlived all the previous cats and still lives under our roof, growing into an impressive feline old lady. A very successful hunter, she spends most summer nights outside. Whenever I hear her in a high-pitched whine, I know not to open the door and let her in. That means she has brought one of her victims to share with us. No thank you, Angel.

Angel has survived several tragedies that should have finished her off. But as we all know, cats have nine lives, and she is on number six or seven.

~ She got a mysterious infection--cured by antibiotics
~ She got bit by a rattlesnake—cured by antibiotics
~ She got stuck up a super tall tree in a snowstorm—rescued by our tree-climbing friend in freezing weather.
Just to name a few.

A family we are close to, at one time, had twenty-nine cats. Yes, I said twenty-nine. They actually lived in a rather nice home with a pool and a beautiful barn. At the time, all four children were ages two to six and the mother collected the cats to keep her children safe from the rattlesnakes that frequented their front yard.

On several occasions, she witnessed the cats surround a snake that had the misfortune of entering their domain and teasing it until they finally finished it off. She said the cats made her feel secure sending her four children outside to play.

Dogs have masters . . . cats have slaves.

Chapter 33

Where Do Cats Go When They Disappear?

In ancient times cats were worshipped as gods;
they have not forgotten this.
~ Terry Pratchett

Our black and white cat, Duchess, was getting along in years, lying around the house and sleeping more. One day she disappeared. I romantically thought she went off into the nearby wild lands to die. Then about a month later, I heard a small, consistent "mew" and couldn't find where it originated. Finally, after searching everywhere, my husband looked under the house. The opening had been nailed shut for the winter and somehow, Duchess got herself locked in. She survived there an entire month without any food or water that we could detect.

Another extraordinary story happened to a family moving to Hawaii. They packed up their belongings into boxes that would be sent the long way by ship. Then, when ready to go, they couldn't find the family cat. After days of searching, they finally determined that the cat sensed the change and left the house. Cats are very good at detecting emotions and seem sensitive to them.

When they arrived in Hawaii, they had to wait a few weeks for their household items to arrive. Then when they unpacked the boxes, there suddenly appeared the cat, neatly shut up inside. Everyone rejoiced to be reunited, especially the cat.

***National Cat Day is always October 29
***National Cat Lady Day is always April 19

Chapter 34

When and Where Were Dogs Domesticated?

*Even the tiniest Poodle or Chihuahua is still a
wolf at heart.   ~ Dorothy Hinshaw*

A study shows that our "best friend" in the animal kingdom may also be our oldest one. All dogs are descended from wolves. Anthropologist, Brian Hare, says, "The domestication of dogs was one of the most extraordinary events in human history."

There is much speculation on where and when it took place. But according to one study, it all started in Southern China, Mongolia and Europe, perhaps as far back as 20,000 to 40,000 years ago. One study shows that the dog/human relationship can be traced back 11,000 years, to the end of the last Ice Age. This confirms that dogs were domesticated before any other known species.

The 2018 movie, *Alpha,* shows this bond when a young hunter-gatherer from the last ice age, 20,000 B.C., befriends an injured wolf. The cinematography of *Alpha* is exquisite.

Scientists remain divided about how dogs became domesticated from wolves. One side suggests that ancient hunter-gatherers used wolves as hunting companions and/or guards, gradually training and taming them. But the other side argues that domestication started later, when wolves stole food leftovers from settlements and began to live alongside people. Perhaps it was a little of both of these theories.

Some propose that the domestication of dogs may have happened several times during history, in many different ways.

Most dog breeds that we recognize today were developed in the last one hundred and fifty years by what's become known as the Victorian Explosion. During this period, dog breeding intensified and expanded, resulting in many of our current dog breeds.

The Victorians, influenced by the ideas of Darwin, became passionate and dedicated to breeding the ideal dog. This sort of emphatic breeding continued throughout the 20th century, resulting in over four hundred types of recognized dog breeds.

The downside of this extensive breeding program is the loss of genetic diversity, which has led to breed-specific health consequences as well as the development of some undesirable diseases. Hence, the argument for embracing the concept of "the mutt."

***National Mutt Day is both July 31 and December 2

Chapter 35

A Dog, A Cat and A Rat

"If they can get along—why can't we?"
~ Gregory Pike

Years ago, we were visiting our parents in Bisbee, Arizona. An amazing small town nestled in the desert foothills of southern Arizona near the Mexico border. It's full of unique characters and a colorful culture.

We were walking up the street, one day, when we came upon an extraordinary sight. A man was sitting on the sidewalk with his dog. But on the dog sat a cat and on the cat, sat a rat. No, I'm not kidding. We were astounded and just stood there staring at the unlikely companions.

The man was a traveler who spent part of his year on the streets of Santa Barbara, California. Wherever he went, so did his three companions, a dog, a cat and a rat.

His traveling companions were his statement for world peace. He said, "If they can get along--why can't we?" Look them up on the internet to see this amazing trio.

Gregory Pike and his furry entourage: Booger, Kitty, and Mousey. Every day he walks around with Booger, the dog, on a leash. On top of Booger sits Kitty, who holds on to the harness around Booger like a saddle. On top of Kitty sits Mousey (who is really a rat), wrapped closely around Kitty's neck. It's obvious the bond between these animals is deep.

They all accept one another as members of the same family, regardless of their species. Gregory has been spreading this message of peace, respect, and tolerance for years, and has become an integral member of Santa Barbara society, known and loved by the community.

Gregory Pike has been studying animal habitats and psychology for about 30 years. He has worked with animal rescues and rehabilitation centers for mountain animals, and has a diverse background in animal training.

2021 Dog, Cat and Pet Holidays

Following is an entire year of dog, cat and pet holidays to give you an idea of how much is going on in the animal world and their owners. Each year the dates will be slightly different. This is to give you an idea of each time period so you can participate or pass the info on.

JANUARY

Month-Long Observances

- **National Train Your Dog Month.**

- **Walk Your Pet Month.**

- **Unchain a Dog Month.**

One-Day Holidays

- Jan. 2: **National Pet Travel Safety Day.**

- Jan. 2: **Happy Mew Year for Cats Day.**

- Jan. 14: **National Dress Up Your Pet Day.**

- Jan. 22: **National Answer Your Cat's Question Day.**

- Jan. 24: **Change a Pet's Life Day.**

- Jan. 29: **Seeing Eye Guide Dog Anniversary.**

FEBRUARY

Month-Long Observances

- **Beat the Heat Month.**

- **Dog Training Education Month.**

- **National Cat Health Month.**

- **Spay/Neuter Awareness Month.** (Humane Society of the United States)

- **Pet Dental Health Month.**

- **Responsible Pet Owners Month.**

- **National Prevent a Litter Month.**

Week-Long Holidays

- Feb. 7-14: **Have a Heart for Chained Dogs Week.**

- Feb. 15-16: **Westminster Kennel Club Annual Dog Show.** Held at New York City's Madison Square Garden, this event is televised. Each breed has an associated rescue group.

- Feb. 23-29: **National Justice for Animals Week.**

One-Day Holidays

- Feb. 3: **Doggie Date Night.**

- Feb. 3: **National Golden Retriever Day.**

- Feb. 14: **Pet Theft Awareness Day.**

- Feb. 20: **Love Your Pet Day.**

- Feb. 22: **Walking the Dog Day.**

- Feb. 23: **International Dog Biscuit Appreciation Day.**

- Feb. 23: **National Dog Biscuit Day.**

- Feb. 25: **World Spay Day.** Annual campaign by the Humane Society International and The Humane Society of the United States; held the last Tuesday of February. Created to combat the crisis of pet overpopulation in every corner of the globe, animal lovers are encouraged to spread the word through social media and help to raise funds for the paws cause.

- Feb. 25: **Spay Day USA.**

MARCH

Month-Long Observances

- **Poison Prevention Awareness Month.**

- **Adopt a Rescued Guinea Pig Month**.

Week-Long Holidays

- March 1-7: **Professional Pet Sitters Week**.

- March 21-27: **National Poison Prevention Week.**

One-Day Holidays

- March 3: **If Pets Had Thumbs Day.**

- March 13: **K-9 Veterans Day.**

- March 17: **Saint Gertrude of Nivelles Day**— patron saint of cats.

- March 23: **National Puppy Day.**

- March 23. **Cuddly Kitten Day.**

- March 28: **Respect Your Cat Day.**

- March 30. **Take a Walk in the Park Day.** Although not exclusively a pet holiday, this day makes a great time to explore a new park with your dog!

APRIL

Month-Long Observances

- **Canine Fitness Month.**

- **Active Dog Month.**

- **National Adopt a Greyhound Month.**

- **National Heartworm Awareness Month.**

- **National Pet First Aid Awareness Month.** This event is an effort by the American Red Cross to draw attention to the need to know specialized pet first aid.

- **Prevent Lyme Disease in Dogs Month.**

- **Prevention of Cruelty to Animals Month.** (ASCPA)

- **National Pet Month.** (UK)

Week-Long Holidays

- April 1-7: **International Pooper Scooper Week.**
- April 1-7: **National Raw Feeding Week.**

- April 11-17: **Animal Care and Control Appreciation Week.** 2nd full week in April.

- April 11-17: **National Dog Bite Prevention Week.** 2nd full week in April.

- April 18-24: **Animal Cruelty/Human Violence Awareness Week.** An effort by the Humane Society of the United States. Third week in April.

- April 18-24: **National Pet ID Week.** Third week in April.

- April 23-29: **National Scoop the Poop Week.**

One-Day Holidays

- ☐ April 3: **Every Day is Tag Day.** Always the first Saturday in April.

- ☐ April 6: **National Siamese Cat Day.**

- ☐ April 8: **National Dog Fighting Awareness Day.**

- ☐ April 10: **National Hug Your Dog Day.**

- ☐ April 11: **National Pet Day.**

- ☐ April 11: **Celebrate Shelter Pets Day.**

- ☐ April 11: **Dog Therapy Appreciation Day.**

- ☐ April 19: **National Cat Lady Day.**

- ☐ April 21: **Bulldogs are Beautiful Day.**

- ☐ April 22: **Earth Day.**

- ☐ April 23: **National Lost Dog Awareness Day.**

- ☐ April 25: **World Veterinary Day.** This event from the World Veterinary Association is always celebrated on the last Saturday in April.

- ☐ April 25: **National Pet Parents Day.** Always the last Sunday in April.

- ☐ April 26: **National Kids and Pets Day.**

- ☐ April 27: **National Little Pampered Dog Day.**

- ☐ April 28: **International Guide Dog Day.** Always the last Wednesday in April.

- ☐ April 30: **Adopt a Shelter Pet Day.**

- ☐ April 30: **National Therapy Animal Day.**

- ☐ April 30: **National Tabby Day.**

- ☐ April 30: **Hairball Awareness Day.** Last Friday in April.

MAY

Month-Long Observances

- **National Pet Month.** (US)

- **National Foster Care Month.**

- **Responsible Animal Guardian Month.**

- **Lyme Disease Prevention Month**.

- **Pet Cancer Awareness Month.** Sponsored by Pet Cancer Awareness and the Blue Buffalo Foundation for Cancer Research. (Also see November events.)

- **Chip Your Pet Month.**

- **National Service Animal Eye Exam.** The American College of Veterinary Optholmologists hosts this annual event when over 300 veterinary ophthalmologists donate their services to provide eye exams to service dogs in the US and Canada during the month of May.

Week-Long Observances

- May 2-8: **American Humane's Be Kind to Animals Week**. This week-long event has been celebrated since 1915. Always the first full week of May.

- May 2-8: **Dog Anxiety Awareness Week**. Founded by Assisi Animal Health.

- May 2-8: **National Pet Week.** Always held the first full week of May by the American Veterinary Medical Association.

- May 3-9: **Puppy Mill Action Week.** An initiative of the HSUS, this week is always scheduled to begin the Monday before Mother's Day.

One-Day Holidays

- ☐ May 1: **National Purebred Dog Day.**

- ☐ May 2: **Mayday for Mutts.** First Sunday in May.

- ☐ May 3: **National Specially-Abled Pets Day.**

- ☐ May 3: **International Doodle Dog Day.** ** *Scheduled for September 25, 2021*

- ☐ May 8: **National Dog Mom's Day.** Second Saturday in May.

- ☐ May 9: **National Animal Disaster Preparedness Day.**

- ☐ May 14: **International Chihuahua Appreciation Day.**

- ☐ May 20: **National Rescue Dog Day.**

JUNE

Month-Long Observances

- **Adopt-a-Cat Month®.** From the American Humane Association.

- **Adopt-a-Shelter-Cat Month.** From the ASPCA.

- **National Foster a Pet Month.** New from the Petco Foundation.

- **National Pet Preparedness Month**. This month, timed for the first month of hurricane season, urges people with pets to make preparations in case they should be hit by a disaster…and that includes making plans for what you would do with your dog in case of a hurricane, tornado, flood or other natural disaster.

- **National Microchipping Month.**

Week-Long Observances

- June 6-12: **Pet Appreciation Week.** First week in June.

- Mid-June: **Animal Rights Awareness Week.**

- June 21-25: **Take Your Pet to Work Week®.**

One-Day Holidays

- June 4: **Hug Your Cat Day.**

- June 8: **Best Friends Day.**

- June 8: **World Pet Memorial Day.** Second Tuesday in June.

- June 19: **National Garfield the Cat Day.**

- June 21: **National Dog Party Day.**

- June 21: **Take Your Cat to Work Day®.**

- June 24: **Cat World Domination Day.**

- June 25: **Take Your Dog to Work Day®.**

JULY

Month-Long Observances

- **National Lost Pet Prevention Month™.** Learn how to keep your pets from becoming lost in this month-long observance launched by PetHub.

- **National Pet Hydration Awareness Month.**

- **Dog House Repair Month.**

Week-Long Holidays

- July 15-18: **Crufts.** Held in Birmingham, England, this is the world's largest dog show, featuring nearly 28,000 canines in its four days.

- July 27-Aug 3: **National Feed a Rescue Pet Week:** Launched in 2017, this holiday by GreaterGood. org and The Animal Rescue Site aims to feed shelter pets.

One-Day Events

- July 1: **ID Your Pet Day.**

- July 4: **Independence Day.** This US holiday is no holiday for dogs; the sounds of fireworks causes many dogs to panic and run, resulting in many lost dogs every year.

- July 11: **All-American Pet Photo Day**.

- July 15: **National Pet Fire Safety Day.** Sponsored by the The National Volunteer Fire Council (NVFC), ADT Security Services and the American Kennel Club® (AKC).

- July 21: **National Craft for your Local Shelters Day.**

- July 21: **No Pet Store Puppies Day.**

- July 26: **National Dog Photography Day.** UK holiday.

- July 31: **National Mutt Day.** Also see Dec. 2.

AUGUST

Month-Long Observances

- **Rawgust.** Celebration of raw feeding for pets for the month of August.

Week-Long Observances

- Aug. 2-8: **International Assistance Dog Week.**

- Aug. 10-16: **Give a Dog a Bone Week.** Hosted by Pets of the Homeless, the event features more than 400 Pets of the Homeless donation sites nationwide asking their community to bring donations of pet food and supplies to assist the pets of the homeless.

One-Day Holidays

- Aug. 1: **DOGust Universal Birthday for Shelter Dogs.** The North Shore Animal League America, the world's largest no-kill animal rescue and adoption organization, declared August 1 as a birthday for all the shelter animals whose birthdays are unknown. Happy DOGust!!

- Aug. 5: **Work Like a Dog Day.**

- Aug. 8: **International Cat Day.**

- Aug. 10: **Spoil Your Dog Day**.

- Aug. 10: **National Lazy Day.**

- Aug. 15: **National Check the Chip Day.** AVMA and the American Animal Hospital Association (AAHA) joined together to create "Check the Chip Day."

- Aug. 16: **Saint Roch's Day.** Patron saint of dogs.

- Aug. 21: **International Homeless Animals' Day.**

- Aug. 17: **National Black Cat Appreciation Day.**

- Aug. 17: **International Nonprofit Day.**

- Aug. 22: **National Take Your Cat to the Vet Day.**

- Aug. 26: **National Dog Day.** One of the most popular pet holidays of the year, we've got an entire page devoted to National Dog Day with ideas on how you and your dog can celebrate together

- Aug. 28: **Rainbow Bridge Remembrance Day.**

- Aug. 30: **National Holistic Pet Day.**

SEPTEMBER

Month-Long Observances

- **Happy Cat Month.** Established by the CATalyst Council.

- **National Service Dog Month.**

- **National Pet Insurance Month.**

- **Responsible Dog Ownership Month.**

- **Pet Sitter Education Month.**

- **Animal Pain Awareness Month.**

- **National Disaster Preparedness Month.** Led by FEMA's *Ready* Campaign, Citizen Corps and The Advertising Council, this effort encourages individuals, families, businesses and communities to work together and take action to prepare for emergencies. Visit Ready.gov.

Week-Long Observances

- Sept. 12-18: **Adopt-a-Less-Adoptable-Pet Week.** Always the third week in Sept.

- Sept. 19-25: **National Deaf Dog Awareness Week.** Last full week in September.

- Sept. 19-25: **National Dog Week.** Last full week in September.

One-Day Holidays

- Sept. 1: **Ginger Cat Appreciation Day**.

- Sept. 8: **National Dog Walker Appreciation Day.** Founded in 2016 by Wag!, this day (always Sept.8) recognizes the work of professional dog walkers.

- Sept. 11: **National Pet Memorial Day.** Established by the International Association Of Pet Cemeteries & Crematories (IAOPCC). Second Sunday in September.

- Sept. 11: **National Hug Your Hound Day.** Second Sunday in September.

- Sept. 13: **Pet Birth Defect Awareness Day**. A day dedicated to the issue of pet birth defects including information on identification, prevention and treatment.

- Sept. 17: **National Pet Bird Day**. A new holiday founded by the Bird Enjoyment & Advantage Koalition (BEAK).

- Sept. 18: **Puppy Mill Awareness Day.** Third Saturday in September.

- Sept. 18: **Responsible Dog Ownership Day.** Always the third Saturday in September.

- Sept. 19: **National Meow Like a Pirate Day.**

- Sept. 23: **Dogs in Politics Day (also known as Checkers Day).** Recognizing the dogs of politicians.

- Sept. 23: **Remember Me Thursday®** Remember Me Thursday® is an international social media awareness day that brings attention to the millions of adoptable pets waiting in shelters and remembers those pets who never got a second chance. Share your rescue pet using #RememberMeThursday.

- Sept. 25: **International Doodle Dog Day.** ** *Originally scheduled for May but rescheduled due to coronavirus.*

- Sept. 26: **World's Largest Pet Walk.** Sponsored by Pet Partners.

- Sept. 28: **World Rabies Day.** Sponsored by the Global Alliance for Rabies Control.

OCTOBER

Month-Long Observances

- **Adopt-A-Dog Month®.** By American Humane Association.

- **Adopt-a-Shelter Dog Month.** By ASPCA.

- **National Animal Safety and Protection Month.**

- **National Pet Wellness Month.**

- **National Pit Bull Awareness Month.**

Week-Long Observances

- Oct. 1-7: **National Walk Your Dog Week.**

- Oct. 3-9: **Animal Welfare Week.**

- Oct. 17-23: **National Veterinary Technician Week.** Sponsored by the National Association of Veterinary Technicians of America.

One-Day Holidays

***Oct. 1: **National Fire Pup Day.**

- Oct. 1: **National Black Dog Day.**

- Oct. 4: **World Animal Day.**

- Oct. 13: **National Pet Obesity Awareness Day.**

- Oct. 16: **National Feral Cat Day.**

- Oct. 17: **National Fetch Day.**

- Oct. 21: **National Pets for Veterans Day.**

- Oct. 27: **National Black Cat Day**

- Oct. 28: **Plush Animal Lovers Day.** A day that most dogs will be happy to celebrate…as they unstuff those plush toys…

- Oct. 29: **National Cat Day.**

- Oct. 30: **National Pit Bull Awareness Day.** Last Saturday in Oct. (unless Halloween falls on the last Saturday, then another date is chosen).

NOVEMBER

Month-Long Observances

- **Adopt a Senior Pet Month.** By ASPCA.

- **National Pet Awareness Month.**

- **National Senior Pet Month.**

- **Pet Cancer Awareness Month.** Sponsored by Veterinary Pet Insurance (VPI) and the Animal Cancer Foundation. (Also see May events.)

- **Pet Diabetes Month.**

Week-Long Observances

- Nov. 1-7: **National Animal Shelter Appreciation Week.** by The Humane Society of the United States. First full week of November.

One-Day Holidays

- Nov. 1: **National Cook for Your Pets Day.**

- Nov. 7: **National Canine Lymphoma Awareness Day.**

- Nov. 17: **National Take a Hike Day.**

- Nov. 25: **National Dog Show.** Always broadcast in the US on Thanksgiving, this event is held at The Greater Philadelphia Expo Center in Oaks, Pennsylvania and is hosted by the Kennel Club of Philadelphia.

DECEMBER

Month-Long Observances

- National Cat Lover's Month.

One-Day Events

- Dec. 2: **National Mutt Day**.
- Dec. 5: **International Volunteer Day**.
- Dec. 9: **International Day of Vet Medicine**.
- Dec. 15: **National Cat Herders Day**.

Mila is the author of six books and has been teaching writing, publishing and public speaking for the past twenty years. Her two programs are very comprehensive, "From Pen to Published" and "Write Your Short Book in a Day". One of Mila's main talents is to make any subject easy, inspiring and accessible for the participant. Mila also offers virtual one-on-one Zoom calls that are very productive. Learn more at MilaJohansen.com.

www.ingramcontent.com/pod-product-compliance
Lightning Source LLC
Chambersburg PA
CBHW050951050726
47592CB00007B/2528